Animals IN and OUT

RiverStream Readers
Animal Antonyms

by Beth Bence Reinke

Ideas for Parents and Teachers

RiverStream Readers let children practice reading informational texts at the earliest reading levels. Familiar words and concepts with close photo-text matches support early readers.

Before Reading
- Discuss the cover photo with the child. What does it tell him?
- Ask the child to predict what she will learn in the book.

Read the Book
- "Walk" through the book and look at the photos. Let the child ask questions.
- Read the book to the child, or have the child read independently.

After Reading
- Use the photo quiz at the end of the book to review the text.
- Prompt the child to make connections. Ask: *What are some other animals that are either in or out?*

Amicus Readers hardcover editions published by Amicus.
P.O. Box 1329, Mankato, MN 56002
www.amicuspublishing.us

Copyright © 2014. International copyright reserved in all countries. No part of this book may be reproduced in any form without written permission from the publisher.

RiverStream Publishing reprinted with permission of The Peterson Publishing Company.

Library of Congress Cataloging-in-Publication Data

Reinke, Beth Bence.
 Animals in and out / Beth Bence Reinke.
    pages cm. -- (Animal antonyms)
 ISBN 978-1-60753-501-0 (hardcover : alk. paper) -- ISBN 978-1-60753-532-4 (eBook)
 1. English language--Synonyms and antonyms--Juvenile literature. 2. English language--Comparison--Juvenile literature. 3. Animals--Juvenile literature. I. Title.
 PE1591.R463 2014
 428.1--dc23
                    2013004496

Photo Credits: Sergey Uryadnikov/Shutterstock Images, cover (top), 16 (bottom middle); Shutterstock Images, cover (bottom), 1 (bottom), 3, 4, 12, 13, 16 (top right), 16 (bottom left), 16 (bottom right); Tom Reichner/Shutterstock Images, 1 (top); Heiko Kiera/Shutterstock Images, 5; Gerald Marella/Shutterstock Images, 6; Cathy Keifer/Shutterstock Images, 7; Kirsten Wahlquist/Shutterstock Images, 8; Leon Marais/Shutterstock Images, 9, 16 (top left); Cheryl E. Davis/Shutterstock Images, 10, 16 (top middle); Henk Bentlage/Shutterstock Images, 11; Ron Smith/Shutterstock Images, 14; Gentoo Multimedia Limited/Shutterstock Images, 15

Produced for Amicus by The Peterson Publishing Company and Red Line Editorial.

Editor Jenna Gleisner
Designer Jake Nordby

In and out are antonyms. Antonyms are words that are opposites. Which animals are in or out?

Baby kangaroos ride in their mothers' pouches.

Baby snakes hatch out of eggs. They each have a little tooth to break their eggs open.

Woodpeckers peck their beaks in trees to eat bugs.

Chameleons stick out their tongues to catch bugs.

Otters swim in water to find food. They can eat in the water while they swim.

Hippos come out of the water to graze.

Baby birds stay in their nest. They are safe in the nest.

Prairie dogs poke out of their holes. They look for danger.

Red foxes and their cubs rest in dens.

Lions sleep out in the open.

Penguins dive into the water to look for fish.

They pop back out onto the ice. They bring fish to their babies.

Photo Quiz

Which animals are in?
Which animals are out?

Photo Quiz

Which animals are up?
Which animals are down?

They dive back down into the sea and swim away.

Some animals can be up and down. Dolphins swim up for air.

Walrus tusks point down. Tusks help walruses climb onto the ice.

Rhinoceros horns point up. Rhinos can charge at lions with their horns.

Otters slide down into water to swim and look for food.

11

Meerkats stand up on their hind legs to watch for danger.

Anteaters dig their snouts down into logs. They catch ants with their sticky tongues.

Elephants lift their trunks up in the air. They spray water up when they take a bath.

Chipmunks dash down into burrows to stay safe.

Red-eyed tree frogs climb up into trees to stay safe.

Fish swim deep down in the ocean.

Eagles fly high up in the air.

Up and down are antonyms. Antonyms are words that are opposites. Which animals are up or down?

Ideas for Parents and Teachers

RiverStream Readers let children practice reading informational texts at the earliest reading levels. Familiar words and concepts with close photo-text matches support early readers.

Before Reading
- Discuss the cover photo with the child. What does it tell him?
- Ask the child to predict what she will learn in the book.

Read the Book
- "Walk" through the book and look at the photos. Let the child ask questions.
- Read the book to the child, or have the child read independently.

After Reading
- Use the photo quiz at the end of the book to review the text.
- Prompt the child to make connections. Ask: *Can you think of other animals that are up or down?*

Amicus Readers hardcover editions published by Amicus.
P.O. Box 1329, Mankato, MN 56002
www.amicuspublishing.us

Copyright © 2014. International copyright reserved in all countries. No part of this book may be reproduced in any form without written permission from the publisher.

RiverStream Publishing reprinted with permission of The Peterson Publishing Company.

Library of Congress Cataloging-in-Publication Data

Reinke, Beth Bence.
 Animals up and down / Beth Bence Reinke.
    pages cm. -- (Animal Antonyms)
  ISBN 978-1-60753-500-3 (hardcover) -- ISBN 978-1-60753-535-5 (eBook)
 1. English language--Synonyms and antonyms--Juvenile literature. 2. English language--Comparison--Juvenile literature. 3. Animals--Juvenile literature. I. Title.
 PE1591.R468 2014
  428.1--dc23
              2013004512

Photo Credits: Rich Carey/Shutterstock Images, cover (bottom); Steve Collender/Shutterstock Images, cover (top front); Adrian Nunez/Shutterstock Images, cover (top back); Eric Gevaert/Shutterstock Images, 1 (top); Ron Rowan Photography/Shutterstock Images, 1 (bottom), 16 (bottom middle); Sebastian Knight/Shutterstock Images, 3 (top), 16 (bottom right); Kristina Vackova/Shutterstock Images, 3 (bottom); Igor Kovalenko/Shutterstock Images, 4, 16 (top left); Natursports/Shutterstock Images, 5, 16 (top middle); Worldswildlifewonders/Shutterstock Images, 6; Margaret M Stewart/Shutterstock Images, 7, 16 (bottom left); Jiri Foltyn/Shutterstock Images, 8, 16 (top right); Jupiterimages/Thinkstock, 9; EcoPrint/Shutterstock Images, 10, 12; Hung Chung Chih/Shutterstock Images, 11; BMJ/Shutterstock Images, 13; Sokolov Alexey/Shutterstock Images, 14; Willyam Bradberry/Shutterstock Images, 15

Produced for Amicus by The Peterson Publishing Company and Red Line Editorial

Editor Jenna Gleisner
Designer Jake Nordby

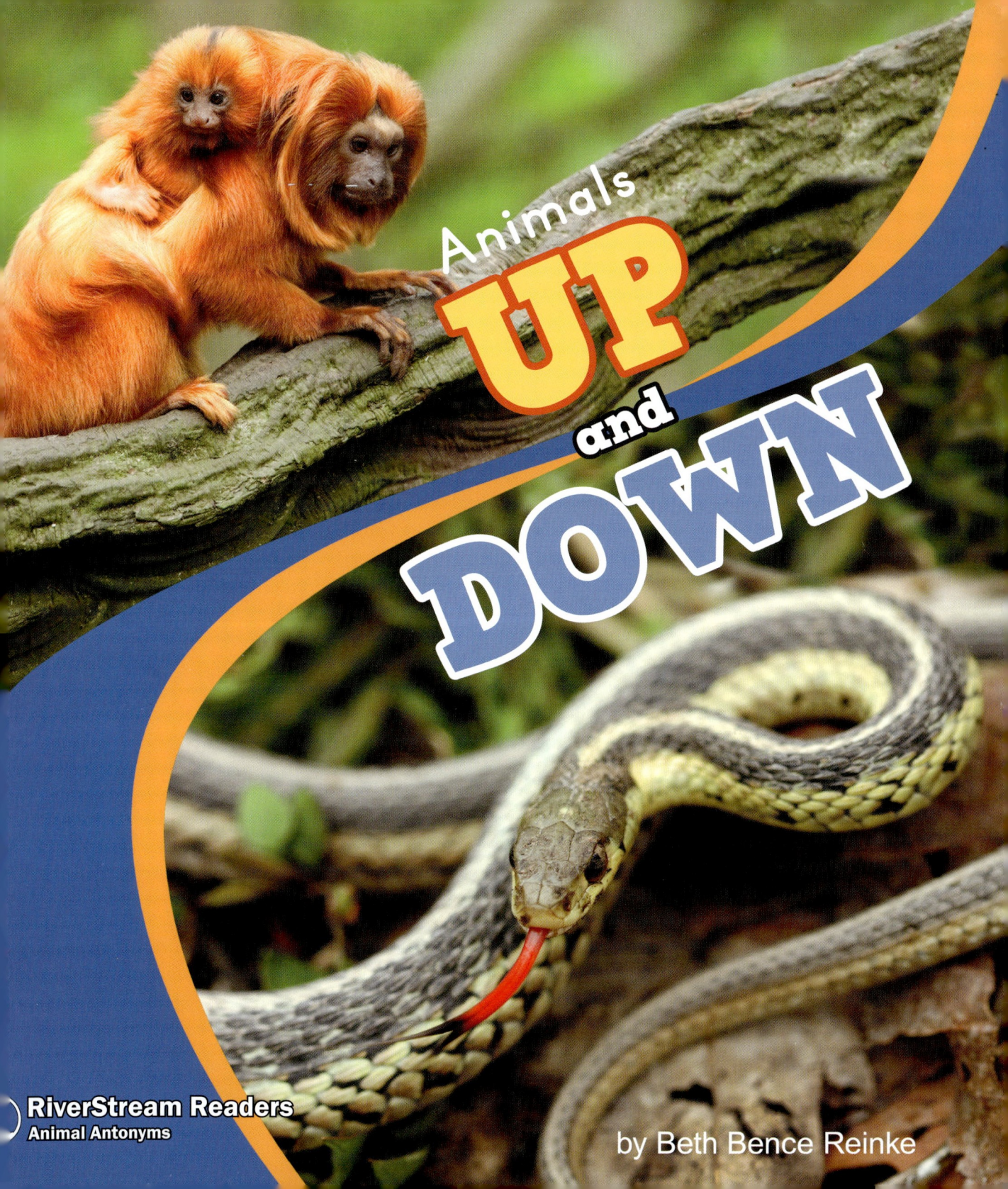

Animals Up and Down

RiverStream Readers
Animal Antonyms

by Beth Bence Reinke